Charity Begins ...

A play

Bettine Manktelow

ALRA
www.alra.co.uk

Samuel French—London
www.samuelfrench-london.co.uk

ALRA
R06621N2685

Please see page iv for further copyright information

CHARACTERS

First produced by The New Deal Theatre Company at St George's Hall, Deal, on 24th February 2006, with the following cast:

Teresa Cowlls	Bettine Walters
Melanie Maple	Coralie Kavanagh
Mrs Castle-Kettle	Pat Hoddinott
Angie	Angela Jeffrey

Directed by Bettine Walters

CHARACTERS

Teresa Cowlls, smart, middle-class woman, smug, self-satisfied, patronizing

Melanie Maple, dowdy, put-upon, downtrodden, more of a loser

Mrs Castle-Kettle, snobbish milady type, patronizing to everybody

Angie, quiet, mousy woman with a big secret; 40-50

The action takes place in office of the Castle Aid Charitable Trust for Women

Time—the present

CHARITY BEGINS ...

The office of the Castle Aid Charitable Trust for Women

There is a desk or table DL with chairs behind and in front of it. There is a filing cabinet UC and another table R. There is a door UR, and an exit between the flats UL

The phone is ringing as the CURTAIN *rises*

Teresa Cowlls, a smart, smug, middle-class, middle-aged woman enters R. She is carrying a wadge of letters, her handbag and her car keys. She stares at the phone in irritation

Teresa Oh, bother! (*She leaves her handbag and keys on the filing cabinet but takes the letters with her, goes over to the phone and picks up the handset. Answering in a very formal, bored voice*) Castle Trust for Women, how may I help you? ... (*She changes her tone and becomes ingratiating*) Oh, Mrs Castle-Kettle. ... How nice to hear from you! I was coming up the stairs when I heard the phone ... I was dawdling, I must admit. ... (*With a false laugh*) Of course I haven't forgotten that you're coming in today. We're going to the opening of the Women's Refuge. We must decide who should make the opening address. ... Oh, you thought *you* would! (*Rather piqued*) I do happen to have made a few notes myself — perhaps we could discuss it. ... Very well! See you soon! (*She puts her things down on the desk with a cross gesture and begins to sort through the post. She finds an interesting letter and sits down to read it*)

There is a knock at the door

Come in!

Melanie Maple enters R. *She is an untidy woman of about forty-five, dressed haphazardly, carrying a shopping bag with some shopping*

Melanie Is this the Castle Trust?

Teresa (*at her most patronizing*) That is so! Do come in! How may I help you?

Melanie I'm Melanie Maple. I've come to volunteer.

Teresa Oh, splendid!

They shake hands across the desk

Teresa Cowlls. I'm the organizer. Do sit down. (*She indicates the chair opposite her own*) How nice of you to drop in. Did the Volunteer Centre send you?

Melanie No, It was my daughter's idea. She thought I needed to get out of the house.

Teresa How thoughtful!

Melanie Not really — I think she just wanted me out of her way!

Teresa Whatever the reason we're awfully glad to have you. Have you had any experience of helping women?

Melanie Only myself, and I haven't been very good at that! (*She sighs*) I was just hoping you'd find me something to do.

Teresa (*glancing at the pile of letters on her desk*) Can you type?

Melanie No.

Teresa Pity. I do need help in the office at the moment. I'm having to answer everything in longhand. It's such a bore! (*She takes the letters and resolutely puts them in a drawer*) Never mind that now!

Melanie You could get a typist from the Job Centre.

Teresa (*horrified*) What! And pay? We couldn't spend the charity's money like that! The committee would never stand for it.

Melanie What committee?

Teresa Our committee. Like most charities we are run on democratic principals. The Social Services representative on our committee is always emphasising the importance of volunteers. Anyone in a high-powered, well-paid job knows the importance of volunteers to do all the things they haven't time to do. There is a great sea of volunteers out there just waiting to be asked to do unpaid work, so they tell me.

Melanie And is there?

Teresa Of course — in theory. It's just in practice we never seem to find them. You haven't been a volunteer before, I take it!

Melanie Only as a housewife. That must qualify for volunteering. It's unpaid.

Teresa Oh, you poor dear! You must have a mean husband.

Melanie *Had*. I'm divorced.

Teresa How unfortunate! We don't ask for details here, but we do draw the line at terrible scandals. I take it there was no terrible scandal?

Melanie (*uncomfortably*) Not a *terrible* scandal, no, just a bit of talk in the Close where I live.

Teresa But not about you!

Melanie (*evasively*) Not really.

Teresa Good! We do have to take care that our volunteers are respectable. I know that's old-fashioned, but we *have* to be old-fashioned. You can hardly give other women advice if you yourself have a shady past — I'm sure you know what I mean.

Melanie (*regretfully*) No, my past isn't a bit shady, I'm afraid.

Teresa You'll have to fill in an application form. (*She looks through the desk drawers hopefully*)

Melanie I could scribble my name and address down any old where.

Teresa But you must fill in the appropriate form. That's a prerequisite of the job — if only I can find one. (*She goes over to filing cabinet and begins to look through it*)

Melanie All right. (*She stands up*) Perhaps I could help you look?

Teresa No, it's all right. It's just such a mess. The filing system needs re-organizing. That's a job in itself! (*Foraging through drawers; over her shoulder*) You see, we do have to be careful about volunteers. I made a dreadful mistake once with a gardener.

Melanie (*intrigued*) Did you?

Teresa (*giving up looking and moving downstage*) Yes, this lovely young man came along offering to do gardening. When I say lovely, I mean lovely! Tall, dark, *very* good looking!

Melanie How old?

Teresa Thirtyish! Very fit! I'm sure he worked out!

They both sigh at their own thoughts

Anyway, I sent him along to a very nice lady who desperately needed help because her husband wasn't any good at it — the gardening I mean. And do you know what happened?

Melanie I'm all agog!

Teresa This very nice lady went and ran off with him.

Melanie What — ran off with the gardener?

Teresa Yes.

Melanie (*enviously*) Oh — how could she?

Teresa And then I discovered that this was something the young man made a habit of — doing the gardening and then running off with an older woman as long as she had a bit of money.

Melanie (*thoughtfully*) I haven't any money. Still I haven't got a garden.

Teresa And her husband was furious with *us,* with *me* for recommending him! You can imagine my embarrassment!

Melanie Yes, I'm sure.

Teresa You see I hadn't checked his credentials — the gardener.

Melanie Oh you should have done that, I think, checked his credentials.

Teresa I should have tried him out myself.

Melanie Of course you should.

Teresa I could have done with it. I'm a widow.

Melanie No husband to do the gardening.

Teresa I'm afraid not, and what's more, my garden was not only bigger than the very nice woman's garden, it was in a much worse state — really neglected. After all, I've been a widow quite a long time!

Melanie (*reflectively*) What a shame!

Teresa Eh?

Melanie (*recollecting herself*) What a shame you didn't find out before you recommended the gardener to that very nice woman, because at least he could have seen to you first.

Teresa Yes, that's what I thought — afterwards. (*She thinks about this regretfully*) However, we all make mistakes. What I am saying now is that we can't be too careful who we take on as volunteers.

Melanie I'm no good at gardening.

Teresa I wasn't suggesting ...

Melanie I'm not much good at anything — that's just the trouble.

Teresa Are you sure you want to volunteer?

Melanie The thing is I can't stand any more.

Teresa Oh, I'm sorry, please sit down!

Teresa ushers Mel into her own chair behind the desk

Melanie No, I don't mean I can't stand *now*. (*She sits down in Teresa's chair*) I used to work in a shop and I stood all the time and I can't do that now.

Teresa (*puzzled*) Why not?

Melanie Varicose veins!

Teresa Oh dear!

Melanie Very painful! And they itch.

Teresa You should have them stripped.

Melanie Sounds horrid! But yes, I know I'll have to have it done. I am on a waiting list but I thought until my name comes up I could fill in the time doing some volunteering, providing I don't have to stand.

Teresa I can see your reasoning, but I'm not sure — (*Looking round the office thoughtfully*) I mean what did you have in mind?

Melanie I thought I'd like to do a bit of visiting, just sitting down and talking to people. I'm good at that — talking to people.

Teresa If all you want to do is chat I think one of the charities for the elderly might suit you better.

Melanie I don't think I'd like that. I worked as a carer once. The old women always talked about their grandchildren and the old men always talked about their bowels. I got fed up with it.

Teresa Yes, I suppose you would, but I'm not sure you've come to the right place. This isn't just a gossiping agency. We supply counsellors ——

Melanie I'm not interested in politics, I'm afraid.

Teresa No, not councillors, counsellors — people who give counselling.

Melanie I see! Advice you mean? Well, I think I'd be good at giving advice, just from my own life ——

Teresa (*quickly*) Oh, don't tell me — but you can't just draw on your own life experiences. Any woman of our age has life experiences to draw upon, marriage, children and so on.

Melanie Yes, I definitely know about marriage, children and so on ...

Teresa But we need to learn how to make the right responses. Take myself for instance. I've been so lucky with my children. They're both at Oxford. My son is studying medicine and my daughter is reading law. I'm very proud of them but it's what I expected, because they were brought up the right way. I can honestly say that they have never caused me a single night's loss of sleep — except when they were babies that is!

Melanie (*enviously*) You *are* lucky!

Teresa So you see drawing on my own experiences I could hardly advise anyone with problem children, could I? Because *my* children haven't been a problem. That's when you have to consult the text book.

Melanie Just to look things up, you mean?

Teresa (*sitting in the chair opposite Melanie*) No, to read, learn and inwardly digest.

Melanie (*doubtfully*) I'm not sure I could inwardly digest.

Teresa That's why you need training! So what about *your* children? What do they do?

Melanie As little as possible. My son doesn't believe in work on principle, he's practising being an anarchist.

Teresa Oh dear!

Melanie And my daughter — well, she's mostly between jobs.

Teresa Where is she now?

Melanie (*looking at her wristwatch*) At this precise moment still in bed I expect!

Teresa You mustn't encourage her to be lazy!

Melanie She doesn't need any encouragement.

Teresa How old is she?

Melanie Seventeen — going on twelve!

Teresa You should push *her* out of the house, not let her push you out!

Melanie But she'd only get up to mischief — whereas I ... (*Woefully*) What can happen to me?

Teresa I understand. (*She rises and moves* R. *Expressing herself*) Volunteering is good for the soul! I'm a volunteer myself — don't look surprised.

Melanie (*not looking surprised*) I'm not!

Teresa I don't *need* to work, financially, but one does feel so bored with the social round. I don't play golf or bridge or anything like that and once the children had flown the nest I felt I had to do *something*.

Melanie (*wistfully*) I suppose the social round could be boring.

Teresa Besides one wants to do something useful with one's life, don't you think? (*Declaiming, taking* C *stage*) The spirit of volunteering is very important to the British character.

Melanie Saves paying anyone.

Teresa And it contributes to so many walks of life! What do you mean saves paying anyone?

Melanie All the volunteers are taking jobs from people who could get paid, aren't they?

Teresa (*coldly*) Not *all* the jobs, only the jobs people don't want.

Melanie Just now you asked me if I could type, so if I could and did it for nothing I'd be taking that job away from someone who needed it, a school leaver, or some poor downtrodden housewife ...

Teresa But think of the Charity! The Charity benefits. We don't pay our workers so the Charity has more money to spend on the clients.

Melanie (*doubtfully*) Does it all go on the clients?

Teresa (*defensively*) Of course! There *are* a few expenses here and there — the odd taxi, the odd lunch, it can't be helped sometimes. Anyway, we digress! (*Sitting opposite Mel*) Now, if you want to volunteer to be a visitor you will have to be trained.

Melanie Oh, why? I said I was good at talking to people but I'm good at listening as well!

Teresa But it isn't just *listening*. There's a difference between listening and listening *properly*.

Melanie Listening properly?

Teresa Of course as a psychiatrist does! Listening intelligently without any criticism.

Melanie Oh, I wouldn't criticize. I'm not perfect.

Teresa (*with determination*) Listening intelligently without gossiping! It's not supposed to be a gossip.

Melanie That might be more difficult.

Teresa And that's where the counselling comes in.

Melanie I see.

Teresa Do you? What do you think we mean by counselling?

Melanie (*hesitantly*) Well, mulling it over in your mind and then saying something like "Never mind, dear, I'm sure it will all work out in the end!"

Teresa (*rising, moving* R) Absolutely not! Mouthing platitudes! That's the worst thing you can do. Never give them false hope! Make them face up to it — whatever it is — and then they can conquer it.

Melanie Give me an example.

Teresa All right. (*Thinking hard*) The other day I had to speak to a woman who came in here complaining that her husband made her feel inferior. I listened to what she had to say and at the end of it I could make a positive judgement.

Melanie What was that?

Teresa I told her she *was* inferior and I urged her to go out and enrol on the Open University or write a book or something — not just sit around moping feeling sorry for herself.

Melanie That must have given her quite a shock!

Teresa No doubt but it must have worked because she didn't come back.

Melanie I'm not surprised.

Teresa I beg your pardon?

Melanie Nothing! I'm just beginning to think perhaps this isn't the right place for me.

Teresa Don't let me put you off. Until you're ready to do visiting I might find you some little job around the office. And there's always the flag day. Since you can't stand for long we could find you a stall where you could sit down, outside the supermarket for instance. Would you like that?

Melanie (*miserably*) I don't know.

Teresa I'll take your particulars anyway. (*Looking on top of the filing cabinet*) Oh, look here's an application form after all. It's only got a few coffee stains on it, but it will do. All you have to do is fill in your name, address, not age — we only ask for a rough assessment of age, between this and that! You don't have to give your age to anyone but the police, did you know that?

Melanie No.

Teresa I do think it's a terrible invasion of privacy to ask a lady her age. So here you are — the main thing we want to know are referees.

Melanie Referees? We don't play games, do we?

Teresa For references, my dear. We must take up references. I told you the mistake I made when I didn't do that — with the gardener.

Melanie (*thoughtfully*) Ah yes! Do you have many volunteers like that? Young men, I mean?

Teresa We hardly ever get young men.

Melanie (*sadly*) That's life, I suppose!

Teresa (*sitting at the desk, looking at the form*) Now, Melanie — you said you were divorced. That goes in here — (*She points to the form*)

Melanie All right.

Teresa Personally, I believe that marriage is indissoluble. I mean the law might divorce you but in the eyes of God you are still married.

Melanie My ex wouldn't like that. That would make his last two kids bastards! Which come to think of it ...

Teresa I was so lucky in my marriage. (*She rises and moves* c) My husband was very successful in business and left me quite well-off. Poor dear, he worked so hard and then dropped dead on the golf course, before he'd reached the nineteenth hole!

Melanie There's no justice!

Teresa At least he died happy in the knowledge that he had left his
wife well provided for!

Melanie Yes, that must have been a great comfort to him!

Teresa Now then, I'll just find some things for you to read, give you
an idea of what we have to deal with. (*She looks for some leaflets
on the table* R) I don't want you to think we are all amateurs. By
no means! We have a team of specialists to counsel our clients on
such things as debt counselling, drug counselling, alcohol
counselling, counselling about runaway children ...

Melanie How do they get their children to run away?

Teresa Pardon?

There is a slight tap at the door

*Mrs Castle-Kettle enters. She is an elderly lady, very domineering
and bossy*

(*With exaggerated delight*) Oh, Mrs Castle-Kettle — Charlotte,
dear! (*She goes up and kisses her cheek*)

Mrs Castle-Kettle I'm a bit late, didn't bring the car today. One can
never park round here.

Teresa I didn't bring the car either. We'll take a taxi — put it down
to expenses.

Mrs Castle-Kettle Of course. (*Looking at Mel*) Who are you?

Melanie (*standing up awkwardly*) I'm just ——

Teresa This is Melanie — er, er — a new volunteer kindly turned
up to offer her services. Melanie, this is Madam Chairman, Mrs
Castle-Kettle, the daughter of the founder of this charity.

Melanie (*in awe*) How do you do.

Mrs Castle-Kettle (*ignoring her and addressing Teresa*) Seeing
her in your place I thought she was taking over! Just as if she
could!

Mrs Castle-Kettle and Teresa laugh heartily

(*To Mel*) So, has our organizer been sorting you out with
something?

Before Mel can answer Teresa does so

Teresa She wants to do some visiting but of course she has to have training first.

Mrs Castle-Kettle Naturally, we all need training. Even I did! And my father started the charity. He was so concerned about women, you see. Very unusual for a man, but he was an unusual man. He was like Gladstone who took to rescuing fallen women, only *my* father wanted to rescue them before they fell!

Melanie (*enthusiastically*) What a good idea!

Mrs Castle-Kettle Quite so!

Mel is about to say something, but Mrs Castle-Kettle turns her back on Mel abruptly

(*To Teresa*) I was so sorry I missed you on Sunday, dear, I went to the early service. I've been so busy this week what with the Parish Council, the Mothers' Union and organizing the Church Fête I haven't had a moment to spare, but I said to my cleaner this morning when she popped in — you know that nice girl who learned all about cleaning by being a volunteer, I said to her I must not neglect my father's charity or there'll be hell to pay!

Melanie (*to herself*) Hell to pay! Oh dear!

Mrs Castle-Kettle (*sharply*) Did you say something?

Melanie (*nervously*) Nothing much. I just meant saying there'll be hell to pay struck me as funny!

Mrs Castle-Kettle (*with a derisory sniff, continuing to Teresa*) So I've made a few notes about what I want to say today. They're bound to ask me to say a few words.

Teresa (*piqued*) I've made some notes, too. We could share it, couldn't we?

Mrs Castle-Kettle (*firmly*) No, dear, I am the Chairman, not you. I am the one to say a few words!

The phone rings. Teresa picks up the receiver sharply: she is cross, but she takes a breath before speaking

Teresa (*putting on her polite voice*) Castle Trust for Women —
how may I help you? ... Oh, Jodie! How lovely to hear from you!
(*To Mrs Castle-Kettle*) It's Jodie!

Mrs Castle-Kettle Oh yes — dear Jodie! (*She turns at once to Mel
and starts talking to her*) I expect Teresa has given you some good
advice. She is very knowledgeable.

Teresa (*into the phone*) I'm so glad you rang! Mrs Castle-Kettle
is here and we have to go to the launch of the new Women's
Refuge ...

Melanie (*to Mrs Castle-Kettle*) Yes, she's told me.

Mrs Castle-Kettle (*sitting in the chair in front of the desk*) As I said
my father was a very charitable person. Everything my dreadful
stepmother said about him wasn't true at all!

Melanie (*uncomfortably*) No? (*She hovers* DL, *not knowing what to
do*)

Teresa (*into the phone*) Oh — *you were* coming over, but darling,
please do come over, because then you can start training our new
volunteer ...

Mrs Castle-Kettle Certainly not! He wasn't that kind of man at all!
Just because he *liked* the company of boys! Of course he did. He
wanted to save them from getting into bad ways, that was all —
and to say a thing like that at the funeral! It was scandalous!

Melanie (*slipping into the chair behind the desk*) It must have been!

Teresa (*into the phone*) You don't know how I'd appreciate it, dear!
She could get started right away. She's *very* keen! ... No experience
as such — but she's the right age — you know what I mean. Past
the first flush ... (*She gives Melanie a quick, bright smile*) Yes —
like us! Ha! Ha!

Mrs Castle-Kettle Fortunately, it didn't get around. I would have
sued her for slander, but by the time she made her denunciation
at the funeral only the relatives were left, and we all knew it was
nonsense!

Teresa (*into the phone*) That's good! I'll tell her! (*She hangs up*)

Mrs Castle-Kettle Of course, she was drunk! So we had to excuse
her. She's dead now anyway!

Melanie (*quite at a loss*) Oh!

Teresa (*cheerfully*) That's good. Jodie is coming over — Jodie Jones, to give you some training, Melanie. She's our very best trainer, isn't she, Charlotte?

Mrs Castle-Kettle Oh yes, she's excellent! Of course she hardly needed any training herself, her husband being a psychiatrist. Some of it must have rubbed off on her.

Melanie (*dismayed*) Do you mean she's coming now? Only I wasn't going to stay much longer.

Teresa Oh, she won't be a sec. She only lives round the corner. You can surely hold the fort until she gets here.

Melanie I wasn't planning to stay.

Teresa But you do want to learn, don't you?

Mrs Castle-Kettle Of course she does! Meeting Jodie Jones! You must make the most of this opportunity, my dear. To be trained by her! I can tell you the CAB couldn't do better!

Teresa Yes, and one excellent thing she does is role-playing. Do you know what I mean?

Melanie Not really!

Teresa She works out little scenarios so that you can imagine what it's like to be a client or a counsellor, or the other way round — really tremendously useful. She used to be an actress so she's awfully good at it.

Melanie It's just that time's getting on. (*She glances ruefully at her watch*)

Mrs Castle-Kettle Still, as Jodie is coming especially to see you it would be terribly rude not to be here.

Melanie (*doubtfully*) I suppose I could stay a little while longer ...

Mrs Castle-Kettle There you are — that's settled. Now then, dear. (*She rises and grabs Teresa's arm*) There's bound to be nothing much to eat so perhaps we could grab a bite afterwards — there's a nice little restaurant I want to try out. It's surely a legitimate expense.

Teresa If you say so, Charlotte!

Mrs Castle-Kettle goes towards the door R

(*Picking up her handbag and keys that she left on the filing cabinet, intermittently to Melanie*) Now you will be all right, won't you? Just sit and read the leaflets and you might just answer the phone and take messages if anyone rings. Otherwise just wait for Jodie, she won't be long, and she'll set you off on the right path. If you want to go before we come back, just slide the catch down — that's all — oh, and make yourself coffee if you like. It's all in the kitchen, just leave fifty p in the little pot.

Mrs Castle-Kettle (*impatiently*) Do come on, dear. I do hate being late unless I have a really good excuse ... and I can't think of one at the moment.

Teresa Yes, I'm coming! See you later!

Teresa and Mrs Castle-Kettle go out R

Melanie goes over and picks up the leaflets Teresa has indicated and looks through them, then puts them down with a frown

Melanie goes out L, *into the kitchen, and can be heard messing about*

There is a timid tap at the door and Angie enters. She looks round nervously and then sits down gingerly in the chair facing the desk

Melanie comes out

Melanie (*seeing Angie*) Oh, hallo — it didn't take you long, did it?
Angie What?
Melanie It didn't take you long to get here!
Angie (*puzzled*) No, not really, once I'd made up my mind.
Melanie I'm Melanie Maple. Pleased to meet you.

Mel takes Angie's hand and shakes it despite Angie's reluctance to do so. There is a pause

I've put the kettle on — would you like a cup of coffee?
Angie No, thank you.

Melanie I do appreciate you coming, really I do, but I wasn't planning to stay long. You don't mind me saying that, do you?

Angie No, of course not. It won't take long — what I have to say.

Melanie Good! I'm looking forward to it. (*She sits down happily at the desk in Teresa's chair and looks across at Angie*)

Angie I don't know where to start. I don't know how to put it into words. It's such a difficult thing asking someone for advice.

Melanie You're asking *me* for advice?

Angie Of course, that's why I came here.

Melanie I thought ——

Angie You are here to give advice, aren't you?

Melanie I should be.

Angie So — would you like to hear my problem?

Melanie Why yes — Oh, I get it. We're role-playing!

Angie We are?

Melanie Good, there's no point in wasting time, is there? Just get on and spit it out and see what I make of it!

Angie Spit it out?

Melanie Whatever is on your mind. You have my full, undivided attention just as a client should have. Is that right?

Angie I suppose so!

Melanie Well?

Angie You see — my husband ...

Melanie Oh, husband trouble! I think there's a leaflet about that! (*She goes over to the small table* R *and picks up a leaflet*) I know about husbands. I used to have one myself. I think I can deal with husbands!

Angie You couldn't deal with this one.

Melanie (*looking at the leaflet*) Is he a gambler? Alcoholic? Does he beat you? Is it another woman?

Angie No, nothing like that.

Melanie He can't be that bad then!

Angie He isn't *bad* at all, not really!

Melanie Then what is wrong with him?

Angie He has these dreadful compulsions.

Melanie Compulsions. Oh, this is a hard one! What does he want to do? Dress up in women's clothes?

Angie Oh no. Not *that* sort of thing. In fact, you'll probably think it's silly!

Melanie No, I won't. (*She sits down again behind the desk*) Try me!

Angie It all began suddenly about two years ago.

Melanie You've put up with it for two years!

Angie Please — let me tell you!

Melanie Sorry — forgot my place for a minute. Go on!

Angie (*standing up to explain*) It began in a very simple way. We were in a garage and I asked him to check the tyre pressures, because I'm never any good at that.

Melanie Neither am I! Oh, sorry!

Angie (*miming checking tyre pressures*) And he started going round checking them very meticulously, getting the pressure right, putting the dust caps back on, getting back into the car, but he'd no sooner got back into the car than he had to get out and do it all over again. This went on for nearly an hour ——

Melanie Heavens!

Angie (*glaring at her*) Until the garage attendant came out and told him he was causing a traffic jam, so we had to go.

Melanie So — why did he do it? Did he tell you?

Angie Yes, he said he couldn't remember which tyre he'd checked first and he kept going round and round to make sure.

Melanie I suppose — the only thing you could do after that was get someone else to check the tyre pressures.

Angie But it wasn't just the car, you see.

Melanie It wasn't? Oh, this is getting good.

Angie No, he started doing it indoors.

Melanie Doing what?

Angie Having compulsions.

Melanie (*really interested*) Heavens, what on earth did he do — compulsively?

Angie Everything ... (*moving downstage, miming the actions to the words*) when he got up in the morning he would stand in front of the mirror combing his hair and then five minutes later he would stand in front of the mirror and comb it again ... and this would go on for at least an hour. He stopped shaving because he couldn't remember whether he'd shaved or not and it made his face sore shaving so many times! I could never let him make a cup of tea because he kept emptying the pot and filling it again and he never knew whether he'd turned the kettle off or not and he had to keep going back to look.

Melanie This is really good! I mean really interesting! I didn't mean to interrupt. Please go on!

Angie (*miming the actions*) If we were watching television in the evening he would think he saw a bit of fluff on his armchair and he would have to brush it off, and after he sat down he'd have to get up again and see if there was any more fluff and he would brush it off again and then he would find a bit of fluff on his trousers and brush that down, and then once he'd sat down he'd stand up and start all over again. This would go on all evening so that I had to stop watching television with him and go in the bedroom! I just couldn't bear it!

Melanie (*mischievously, entering into the spirit of the game*) Oh dear! So what about the bedroom? I hope he wasn't compulsive in the bedroom.

Angie Oh — he was!

Melanie Do tell me!

Angie (*miming the actions*) Before he got in bed he would have to straighten out the sheet and then once he'd got in bed he'd have to get out and straighten it again, usually this went on four or five times. After that he had to shake the pillow up and after he'd got in bed he'd get out and shake it up again! I tell you it was too much for me. I went and slept in the spare room in the end. I couldn't bear it!

Melanie (*mock sincerity*) I am sorry for you — really I am!

Angie I got so tense. I was always waiting for him to do something odd. I couldn't bear friends to call — or even relatives. I could see what a struggle he had trying not to do something compulsively and as soon as they'd gone he'd be off ——

Melanie Off?

Angie Off. (*Quite frenetic this time, rushing around miming tidying up*) Doing something that he'd avoided doing while they were there! Running round tidying up, straightening cushions, straightening chairs, straightening ornaments, anything you could think of and once he'd straightened them up he'd go back and do it all over again! Oh, I can't tell you all of it, it would take me all day! I just got to the point when I wanted it to stop. I suppose I would have done anything for it to stop.

Melanie (*trying not to laugh*) Did you tell anyone about it? Your doctor or anyone?

Angie No, how could I? I'm telling you now and you just think it's funny! Nobody understands.

Melanie I don't think it's funny, not really! (*But she has a job to keep a straight face*) I think it's very clever.

Angie Clever?

Melanie I don't know how you made it up!

Angie I haven't made it up! (*She stands up in indignation*) You won't think I made it up if you know what I did next!

Melanie Go on — shock me!

Angie We were in the kitchen this morning after breakfast and I knew I'd turned the gas taps off, but he started going round checking them while I was trying to eat my breakfast. (*She mimes turning off the gas taps*) He sat down and got up and went to check them not once but a dozen times, and suddenly I just erupted!

Melanie (*enthralled*) What did you do?

Angie I hit him on the head with a frying pan!

Melanie Oh, you didn't!

Angie Yes, I hit him on the head with a frying pan! Like the song! (*She begins to sing, deadpan to the calypso tune as she stands facing audience*) I hit him on de 'ead wid a frying pan, hit him on de 'ead wid a flying pan, hit him on de 'ead wid a frying pan, I killed nobody but my husband.

Melanie (*amazed*) Oh, you're so good!

Angie (*warming to her song*) He's stone-cold dead in de market, he's stone-cold dead in de market, he's stone-cold dead in de market, I killed nobody but my 'usband. (*Having finished singing she turns to Melanie*)

Melanie (*applauding*) You killed him, well done!

Angie Do you really think so?

Melanie Of course! (*She comes round to desk to her*) I tell you what
— you're a very good actress.

Angie I wasn't acting oh, you mean, the song. It just seemed
appropriate.

Melanie I must congratulate you! I don't suppose I'll ever have a
client like this but it's been great fun and I hope I'll learn from it.
Thank you, Jodie! (*She holds out her hand*)

Angie (*not taking her hand*) Who's Jodie?

Melanie Now, don't pretend any longer. I knew right away who
you were. They told me you were coming in, and told me about
the role-playing. I must say I didn't expect you to be quite so
clever, but I have enjoyed it!

Angie I don't know what you're talking about! I felt I had to tell
someone so I thought I'd come here. I can't afford a solicitor. Do
you believe me or not?

Melanie I think you were very convincing, but you don't have to
go on pretending. Of course I believed you!

Angie (*relieved*) Good! I just wanted to try it out on somebody. I
feel much better now. (*She turns away towards door* R)

Melanie (*puzzled*) Where are you going?

Angie I suppose I'll have to go to the police. I've got to get someone
to take the body away. He's really messed up the kitchen bleeding
all over the place. It will take me hours to clean it up. The trouble
is once I start I have to clean it up five or six times over. That's
what I'm like. I'm glad I spoke to you. It's got it off my mind. I'll
go now.

Angie goes off

*Melanie stands in a daze staring ahead of her. The phone rings.
Mechanically she picks it up*

Melanie Hallo — yes, this is the Castle Trust for Women. ... No,
I'm just a volunteer. ...Oh — yes, Jodie Jones? But you were here,
just a moment ago! ... You didn't come. You were delayed! (*She
rises and stares across at the empty chair opposite her*) But —

someone was here ... a woman. I don't know who, I thought it was
you! (*She walks to* c *with the hands-free phone*) She told me a lot
of things. ... No, it wasn't boring! Quite the contrary — I haven't
got over it yet — it was all about ... What? ... It should be
confidential! Well, I suppose it *is* confidential! ... You don't want
to hear? ... Well, what am I supposed to do? ... Go home! Yes,
come to think of it — that is a good idea! ... Will I come back? Oh,
I don't think so ... I don't think I want to be a volunteer now, thank
you very much! Good-bye! (*She hangs up with relief*)

BLACK-OUT

FURNITURE AND PROPERTY LIST

On stage: Desk DL. *On it*: hands-free phone, blotter, in-tray, pens
2 chairs
Filing cabinet. *On top*: application form
Table R. *On it*: various advice leaflets

Off stage: Wadge of letters, handbag, car keys (**Teresa**)
Shopping bag containing shopping (**Melanie**)
Handbag (**Mrs Castle-Kettle**)

Personal: **Melanie**: wristwatch

LIGHTING PLOT

Property fittings required: nil
Interior. The same scene throughout

To open: General interior lighting

Cue 1   **Melanie** hangs up the phone with relief   (Page 20)
           Black-out

EFFECTS PLOT

Cue 1 To open (Page 1)
         Phone

Cue 2 **Mrs Castle-Kettle**: " ... to say a few words!" (Page 11)
         Phone

Cue 3 **Melanie** stands in a daze staring ahead of her (Page 19)
         Phone

Printed by The Kingfisher Press, London NW10 7AS